Monika

Rabbits

**A Complete
Pet Owner's Manual**

Everything about
Purchase, Care, Nutrition,
Grooming, Behavior, and
Training

Photographs: Monika Wegler

Drawings: György Jankovics

Translated from the German
by Helgard Niewisch, D.V.M.

BARRON'S

CONTENTS

THE TYPICAL
DWARF RABBIT

- **Quiet and sociable**

- **Quick, agile, and eager to play**

- **Loves hiding places, caves, and its little house inside the cage**

- **Chewing and nibbling are favorite pastimes**

- **Loves being cuddled**

- **Matures early and is highly reproductive**

More so than most other species, rabbits have managed to keep their original traits as they evolved into pets. This is most obvious when you watch your rabbit at play or while it interacts with others. Rabbits display exuberance and joy when they play catch with each other, kicking up their legs in sheer delight. When rabbits are familiar with each other, they cuddle up and groom each other. How amusing to watch your rabbit sit up to "secure" its environment. At the slightest suggestion of danger, all the rabbits disappear with lightning speed into their house. Tame rabbits will eat right out of your hand and jump up onto your sofa to get their quota of cuddling time.

DECISION MAKING

1 Rabbits need to run free every day for good health.

2 If you have no outdoor facilities, you need to be willing to put up with occasional rabbit droppings on the floor and the chance of chewed furniture.

3 If the rabbits are to live outdoors year-round, they require weather-tight housing and a safely fenced play area. This can be costly.

4 Indoor rabbits, particularly the larger breeds, require extra-large cages. Such cages can be expensive and they take up quite a bit of space in your living area.

5 Rabbits live for eight or more years, which requires a long commitment on your part. Inconvenience should never be the reason to take your rabbit to an animal shelter.

6 Do you have other pets that might not be compatible with a new rabbit (see page 22)?

7 While the actual care of a rabbit is not demanding, it is essential to plan daily interaction if you want truly tame pets.

8 If the rabbit is intended as a child's pet you should be prepared to teach your child the right way to care for the animal, and then be prepared to do it yourself after all.

9 Before you buy a rabbit make sure that no one in the family is allergic to rabbit hair.

10 Who will take care of your rabbit while you are on vacation (see page 30)?

One or a Pair?

While hares are solitary animals, the sociable wild rabbit lives in close-knit colonies. For this reason pet rabbits are happier living in pairs or small groups. Single rabbits require more attention, but the human companion can never quite replace a true mate.

Who Is Compatible with Whom?

✔ Until the age of about three months rabbits have no problem getting used to each other. Siblings from the same litter are the best choice for group living.

✔ Pairs make good companions too, as long as you have the buck neutered as soon as possible. If the doe gets pregnant, what would you do with the pups (see page 10)?

✔ As a rule, two does get along well with each other.

✔ The same is true for neutered bucks; however, intact males will become aggressive as soon as they are sexually mature.

✔ Older animals must get acquainted slowly and gently (see page 19).

PREPARATION AND PURCHASE

Rabbits make friendly and happy companions. They come in a variety of sizes, colors, and length of fur. Large or small, they all need the right housing and care to be healthy and content.

Origin and History

When you look at a giant breed of 15 pounds (7 kg), it is hard to imagine that all rabbit breeds have evolved from the same little wild rabbit (*Oryctolagus cuniculus*).

The history of rabbits contains many errors: Around 1100 B.C., Phoenician seafarers misnamed these animals when they discovered them on the Iberian Peninsula. The Phoenicians thought that they were a species that they had seen on cliffs in their home country, and called them "i-shepan-im," which, although incorrect, was accepted by the Romans. Then the Romans transferred the name into their vocabulary, which resulted in the Latin name Hispania for Spain.

Another error is that rabbits were originally classified as rodents. When you watch rabbits chew on wood you might well agree with this notion, but both the hare (lepus) and the rabbit belong to the family of *lagomorphs*. That is just about all they have in common; in fact, hares and rabbits are very different in their appearance and behavioral traits and they cannot produce offspring together.

Rabbits as Farm Animals and as Pets

Today, most domesticated wild animals live as well-loved and cared-for pets with human companionship. Among these are cats, dogs, cockatiels, and hamsters, to name a few. Rabbits, however, rarely are blessed with human protection and love. The main reason may be the rabbit's ideal characteristics as a food animal: It is highly reproductive, demands little care, adjusts easily, and never voices complaints. Rabbits produce meat and wool and serve as research animals in countless laboratories.

It is truly a lucky rabbit that gets adopted by a pet lover. In order to perpetuate this luck one needs to care for the animal responsibly, in good health, and according to the particular needs of this species.

The elegantly sleek and temperamental Belgian hare.

Where to Buy a Rabbit

✔ Pet stores sell mostly dwarf rabbits and small mixed breeds.

✔ The best source for vendors of recognized breeds is the local or regional breeder association (see page 62).

✔ If you can't find a local source, ask your pet store for help, or check the Internet.

✔ Newspapers usually carry ads from private rabbit fanciers in the classified section.

✔ Animal shelters may offer older but no less gentle and lovable animals for adoption.

The Right Age

Do not accept an animal that is younger than seven weeks; you would not do yourself nor the rabbit a favor. Time and again I have seen animals offered for sale at three to four weeks, which is cruel because these pups should still be nursed by their mother. These animals are excessively stressed by premature weaning and by the change of environment, and the result is a severely compromised immune system and a high incidence of illness.

Male or Female?

Bucks tend to become increasingly restless when they reach sexual maturity; therefore a male rabbit should be neutered unless he was bought specifically for breeding purposes. An intact male will try to mate objects, and will leave urine scent markings everywhere. Eventually, the frustrated animal may suffer. Veterinarians will neuter rabbits at four to six months. Subsequently, bucks will develop balanced and friendly behavior that is suitable for single as well as for group housing.

Does should also be spayed unless they are intended for breeding. When does are in heat they may display aggressive behavior toward their cagemates. Be prepared for this and provide space to separate the animals for a short time. My own does have never fought seriously, their ranking order having been established at

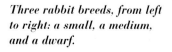

Three rabbit breeds, from left to right: a small, a medium, and a dwarf.

an early stage. Only rarely would a wild chase take place; however, these chases never resulted in injuries.

Health and Personality Traits

If you want to know how to choose a tame rabbit, watch one with the pet store handler or breeder—if the rabbit allows the human to handle it without struggling in panic, it's right for you. However, if you see an animal that retreats into the corner of the cage at the sound or sight of a human, it will need a long period of adjustment. Many such animals remain fearful for the rest of their lives. A healthy rabbit is alert, lively, and interacts with its cagemates.

This rabbit is visibly enjoying its outing in the yard.

1. The coat should be smooth and glossy, without bald or scaly areas.
2. The eyes should be bright and clear, never dull. Secretions, redness, or swelling may be signs of disease.
3. The teeth should be aligned as shown on page 33.
4. The ears must be clean without deposits inside or discharges outside.
5. The nose must be dry, with no sneezing or discharge.
6. The vent area must be clean and dry; no

matted hair or fecal soiling.

Note: Never buy a rabbit that has had contact with sick rabbits; the risk of infection is very high.

History of Breeds

As early as Roman times rabbits, mostly wild breeds, were kept as food animals in large walled pens. Later, during the Middle Ages, rabbits became domesticated farm animals. With time they became tamer. Not until the sixteenth century are there records describing a variety of fur colors and sizes unlike those of the wild breeds.

Over time, the wild rabbits changed more and more under the influence of humans and through selective breeding. Not only did wild rabbits become larger and undergo a change in their original protective gray-brown coat color, but their behavior and anatomical features also changed over the years. Rabbits with certain characteristics, such as those with longer fur, were used as breeding animals. It wasn't until the beginning of the twentieth century, in America, that breeding for specific genetic traits got underway. Today there are well over 100 known breeds of rabbits. The ever-increasing color, size, and fur variations make it difficult to count them all. Recognized breeds vary from country to country. Even if you are not interested in breeding your rabbit, you should be informed about the different types of rabbit breeds.

A longhaired Jamora rabbit with her four-week-old off-spring.

Pedigreed Rabbits

A purebred strain of rabbits is characterized by specific traits that are predictably reproduced in the offspring. The "standard" is the model of perfection around which all breeders try to model their stock. The breed standard sets the guidelines for the breeding of purebreds and for their judging at shows. When pedigreed rabbits are judged at a show, they are compared to the ideal for their breed, the ideal being 100 points. Rabbits are judged according to different criteria such as type and body form, weight, coat, structure of head, ears, color and marking, and appearance. They receive a set number of points for each criterion. Recognition of rabbit breeds and registration of individual animals is governed by the American Rabbit Breeders Association (ARBA, see page 62).

Pedigreed rabbits are identified by tattoos, which indicate the letters and numbers that determine the genetic traits of the animal. Pedigreed rabbits get tattooed in both ears. The head of a rabbit fanciers' association undertakes the tattooing no later than the rabbit's third month of life. In the United States, the tattoo in the right ear is the rabbit's registration number. The tattoo in the left ear is the breeder's identification mark for that individual animal.

Rabbit Breeds according to Size and Hair Type

Normal Hairs

LARGE BREEDS
Giants	12–15 lb (5.5–7 kg) or more
Giant, spotted	12–14 lb (5.5–6 kg) or more
Lops	10–12 lb (4.5–5.5 kg) or more

MEDIUM BREEDS
New Zealand Red	6 1/2–10 lb (3–4.5 kg)
Belgian Hares	6 1/2–9 lb (3–4.25 kg), photo page 8
Thuringian	6 1/2–9 lb (3–4.25 kg)

SMALL BREEDS
Saxony Gold	5–7 1/2 lb (2.25–3.5 kg), photo page 15
Deilenaar (Dutch breed)	5–7 1/2 lb (2.25–3.5 kg), photo page 5
Silver, small	4 1/2–7 lb (2–3.25 kg), photo page 15
Dutch	4 1/2–7 lb (2–3.25 kg), photo page 14
Small Chinchilla	4 1/2–7 lb (2–3.25 kg), photo page 15
Fawn	4 1/2–7 lb (2–3.25 kg), photo page 40

DWARF BREEDS
Dwarf Lops	3–4 1/2 lb (1.5–2 kg), photo page 14
Ermine	1 1/2–3 lb (0.7–1.5 kg), photo page 14
Dwarf, color	1 1/2–3 lb (0.7–1.5 kg), photo page 14

Breeds by Type of Fur

SHORTHAIRS
Rex	5–11 lb (2.25–5 kg), photo page 2
Dwarf Rex	1 1/2–3 lb (0.7–1.5 kg)

LONGHAIRS
Angora	6–12 lb (2.5–5.5 kg)
Fox	6–10 lb (2.5–4.5 kg)
Jamora	3–5 lb (1.5–2.25 kg), photo page 12
Dwarf Fox	1 1/2–3 lb (0.7–1.5 kg)

BY HAIR TYPE
Satin	5–9 lb (2.25–4.25 kg)

Normal Hair
Most breeds of rabbits belong to this group. The fur resembles that of wild rabbits. It is smooth and lies flat, and consists of the undercoat, the slightly longer topcoat, and the guard hairs: 1–1 1/2 inches (2 1/2–4 cm) long.

Shorthairs
Hair stands straight out from its base; topcoat and guard hairs are of the same length—about 5/8 of an inch (16 mm) long. This fur is as soft as velvet to the touch.

Longhairs
Angora: Fluffy and wavy fur (at least 2 1/2 inches [6 cm] long).
Fox: Silky smooth fur (2–2 1/2 inches [5–6 cm] long).
Jamora: Fluffy fur, a little less silky than Angora (1 1/2–2 1/2 inches [4–6 cm] long).

Hair Type
Satin: Thick, soft fur made of fine hair strands reflecting a satinlike luster (1–1 1/2 inches [2 1/2–4 cm] long).

Note: The column at left indicates minimum and maximum weights. In addition to the breeds with erect ears, there are breeds with drooping ears, which are called Lops.

P O R T R A I T S :
TYPES OF RABBITS

The various breeds of rabbits are distinguished by size, body structure, coat length, color, and type of fur. The best place to
admire their beauty is at a rabbit show.

*This dwarf
breed is sitting
up to survey
its environ-
ment.*

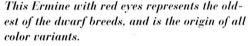

*This Ermine with red eyes represents the old-
est of the dwarf breeds, and is the origin of all
color variants.*

*All rabbits with droopy ears are called
Lops. This photo shows a white
Thuringian Dwarf Lop.*

*Black-and-white Dutch rabbit, belonging to the
small breeds. These animals are lively and display beautiful color markings.*

Saxony Gold rabbits are of compact body type, their fur a deep russet. Their behavior is calm and placid.

This small Chinchilla breed was named after the rodent of the same name from South America.

Small Silver breeds, here shown in silver-black, are very lively. All color variations have white-tipped guard hairs.

The attractive fawn breeds can be bred in black, brown, and blue (this photo).

A Home Indoors

Rabbits are not demanding when it comes to caging, but ample space is essential.

Pet stores carry a variety of cages made of metal and plastic. Solid plastic tops are not recommended because they retain too much heat. Floor space of 20 x 35 inches (51 x 89 cm) is required for one or two dwarf rabbits or for one small-breed animal. Medium-size breeds need at least 25 x 45 inches (64 x 115 cm). The higher the floor pan, the less bedding the rabbit will throw over by digging and jumping; 8–10 inches (20–25 cm), depending on the breed size, should be high enough.

Zinc-covered cage bars are more suitable than plastic-coated bars. The bars should be placed on the upper edge of the bottom tray. This will prevent bedding from sticking to it

This large-size Dalmatian Rex requires an extra-large cage.

when you pick it up. Make sure that the sides of the uppper part of the wiring are well reinforced. There is some very unstable top cage wiring on the market that can collapse when you take it off.

The front should have a door to let the rabbit in and out, and the top should be hinged to allow easy access to the animal and to the furnishings.

Note: Stainless steel top grates are preferred. Plastic-coated grates can be harmful because rabbits chew on them. Remember to get spare clamps to hold the top to the pan; they break easily.

A Hutch Built for Comfort

Rabbits love to hide for privacy when they need rest or protection. Pet stores carry a variety of wooden and plastic nest boxes. A flat top is preferable because rabbits like to sit on top to survey their neighborhood. A floor space of 10 x 15 inches (25 x 38 cm) is sufficient for one adult dwarf rabbit or for two youngsters; 10 x 16 inches (25 x 41 cm) is suitable for grown small breeds. The height should allow a seated animal to have its ears erect without touching the top, and be low enough to fit the animal comfortably between the box and the cage grates.

Food and Water Bowls

Food bowls must be able to withstand chewing and pushing. Plastic or stainless steel bowls turn over too easily; plastic also gets gnawed on. An edge turned inward will help to keep the food from falling out. Glazed stoneware is preferable for pellets and greens. Feed youngsters from small bowls because they like to sit inside larger bowls and will then soil the food.

Self-dispensing feeders keep the food clean, but be careful not to overfeed. It is helpful to hook the dispenser onto the cage bars to keep the food from getting soiled by urine or excrement.

Water bottles with a nipple that hold 1 pint (450 cc) of water will quench even the biggest thirst. It is essential that rabbits have fresh drinking water available at all times. Choose a plastic bottle with a spherical outlet in the water dispenser tube; this keeps water from dripping into the cage.

The hay rack holds the daily hay ration. Pups and youngsters should eat hay from bowls because they could get hurt in racks while trying to jump or play in them. There are various types of hay racks available at your pet supply store.

Checklist
Equipment

1 Indoor cage with a floor space that fits the size and number of animals (page 16). The top is made of metal, and the bedding pan is high enough to keep the litter inside the cage.

2 Low nest box to sleep and hide in; plastic or wood (photo below).

3 Food bowls, water bottle, hay rack.

4 Bedding: straw or shavings. Recommended: soft wood chips to absorb the urine, with one thick layer of straw on top.

5 Litter box that contains cat litter.

6 Comb and brush for grooming.

7 Nail clipper.

8 Branches and toys to chew on (page 37).

Choosing the Right Location

You should choose a suitable location for the cage before you bring the animal home.

For the first free trip around the room, a litter box should be available (see Housebreaking, pages 30 and 31).

✔ Rabbits prefer cool temperatures ranging from 54 to 72°F (12 to 22°C).
✔ Rabbits like bright and airy conditions but cannot tolerate the blazing sun. Therefore, never place the cage close to a heater or in direct sunlight.
✔ Large cages are most secure on the floor. If there is too much draft, place a thick mattress under the pan or find a different area.
✔ Rabbits have highly sensitive hearing. They do not appreciate a location where they are exposed to a loud television, screaming pet birds, or continual human traffic.

Dandelion leaves and other treats are the best aids in taming your new friend.

Helping Your Rabbit Adjust

Transporting your rabbit is very stressful for the animal, and you need to give it time to recover alone in its cage. Keep all other pets away from the newcomer. Too many new things at once will only cause unnecessary stress for the rabbit. You must explain to your child that the rabbit needs a few quiet days to adjust and that it is not yet time to carry it around. It is a good idea to have the breeder or pet shop give you some of the foot that the rabbit has been eating; this will make adjusting to its new home somewhat easier. When the rabbit begins to eat and drink, and to groom itself afterward, and then stretches out in the cage bedding, it has come through the initial shock successfully.

Creating Trust

1. Always approach the cage slowly, addressing the animal in a soothing voice; quick movements and loud voices frighten rabbits.
2. For the first interaction place yourself at eye level with the rabbit on the floor. Wait until the animal approaches the grid; if it appears calm, hold out a treat through the bars.
3. Never try to grab a rabbit suddenly from above, as a predator bird would. Always let the animal sniff your hand first, then calmly lift it out of its cage with both hands.
4. Fully adjusted rabbits love to be petted. Scratch your rabbit behind the ears, and stroke it gently along the entire back.
Note: Rabbits do not tolerate being scratched under the chin or on their belly.

Keep excursions on separate schedules until a friendship is established.

This Dalmatian Rex defends her cage (territory) from the "intruding" competitor.

As long as animals show aggressive behavior they are not ready to be cagemates.

Getting Two Rabbits to Become Friends

Rabbits enjoy living together, but only if they know each other well. Strangers to their territory are immediately attacked and forced to take flight. If you did not acquire two rabbits at the same time, you need to get them used to each other gradually. The younger they are, the sooner you will succeed. If your rabbit has been living alone and is now going to have company, then follow these basic procedures.

✔ Above all, the newcomer needs to have quiet time alone in its cage to get used to the new home. This also serves as a quarantine period (see page 53).

✔ Never put the strage rabbit into the other's cage without making preparations for the introduction, or there could be nasty consequences. During the first two or three weeks place the cages in visual, but not physical, contact.

✔ Gradually move the cages closer to each other until the animals can sniff each other's scent. When each feels safe, they will learn to tolerate the other.

✔ The next step is to let the rabbits have separate free runs. Begin to let one rabbit out of the cage while the other remains in its cage. Don't let them have free runs together until neither rabbit jumps up on its cage bars in an attempt to bite at the other one. This can sometimes take weeks or months to accomplish. If they stay friendly at this stage you can try to put them together for short periods.

✔ For the next step you need to rub onion or garlic all over both animals, particularly in the anal and groin areas, to make them both smell alike. Place both animals in a neutral space where they can run freely, and where no other rabbit's scent could entice them to fight.

✔ With a little luck and patience the encounter should turn into friendship; however, if they start to fight, they will have to live separately.

DAILY MANAGEMENT AND CARE

Rabbits are social and lively pets. Daily opportunities to run free, loving care, and excellent nutrition make happy and healthy animals.

Rabbits and Children

While love and attention are essential for the well-being of rabbits, it is most important to explain to children that they need gentle, slow time to settle in (pages 18–19, Acclimation). This is not the right time to hug, cuddle, and carry the animal around, or to present it proudly to all their friends, including carting it around in a doll carriage.

Parents must teach their kids *how to handle their pet correctly.* Children should be at least of school age before they are given a rabbit as a pet. Only then will they be able to understand how to meet the animal's daily needs. Children will learn to assume responsibility for their pets only by following the consistent behavior and proper role model of the parents. Make it your duty as parents to guide your children into living with and caring for their new pets.

Instructions should begin on the first day; better yet, prepare in advance by teaching proper care even before the animal is brought home. Children need to understand the special needs of these animals if a bonding relationship is to succeed.

Important Rules
✔ Do not disturb your rabbit while it eats or sleeps.
✔ Contrary to electronic toy pets, your rabbit does not sound an alarm when it is hungry or thirsty. While children should be responsible for their pets' care, parents must always check that proper care is being provided.
✔ If the cage is intended for a child's room, the child must understand that loud music and other noises will frighten the rabbit.
✔ Rabbits need exercise and play during their daily outings (pages 50–51). The bed is not the right place; rabbits will urinate on the bed and bite holes in pillows.
✔ When talking to the rabbit, always speak in a calm and gentle tone.
✔ To prevent falls and injuries, rabbits must be picked up and held correctly (page 32).
✔ No chocolate cookies for your rabbit! They will make the rabbit sick.

The rabbit won't jump and hurt itself if you hold it close like this.

A Guinea Pig as Cagemate

As a rule, guinea pigs and rabbits make good companions, as they both are social animals and will rest in close contact and groom each other. The problem arises when the rabbit tries to chase the guinea pig, bites it, or tries to mount it repeatedly. At the onset of sexual maturity (at approximately three months of age) a male rabbit will try to mount a guinea pig. Male rabbits have a powerful sex drive and they do not limit themselves to their own species. The guinea pig is defenseless in this situation. Rabbits must be neutered to live with cagemates (page 10). If your veterinarian thinks that the rabbit is still too young for neutering, then you will have to keep it in a separate cage until it is old enough to be neutered. Approximately four weeks after neutering has taken place, you should be able to put the two animals back in with each other again.

If a doe behaves too aggressively during her heat, the guinea pig must have its own nest box for protection. The box must be small enough to allow only the guinea pig to enter, not the rabbit. Despite all possible problems, the advantages of the two animals living in companionship outweigh the disadvantages of single life.

Getting Along with Cats and Dogs

Once the rabbit is tame and comfortable in your home, you can begin the slow process of getting it used to a dog or cat.

Naturally quiet and tame, rabbits have the *best chances of becoming comfortable quickly.* The genetic dispositions of dogs are even more important, since hunting dogs are naturally more difficult to adjust than a quiet breed. Also, a relaxed Persian cat will be less eager for a chase than a cat that is used to hunting rodents outdoors. Even if such cats show tolerance toward the rabbit, it would be a mistake to leave them alone unsupervised. Remember that dogs and cats are natural predators of rabbits. In addition, there are communication gaps between the animals because of the completely different behavior patterns of dogs, cats, and rabbits. Young animals are the ideal candidates for getting used to each other because they can still be more readily molded and trained.

Harmony among the different species cannot be taken for granted.

Helping the Adjustment Process:

1. Keep the rabbit and the dog or cat in separate rooms until the rabbit has become trusting. Pet the animals lavishly before you introduce them to each other, allowing them to smell each other's scent on your hands.

2. For the first visit keep the rabbit in the cage. Keep the dog on a leash, sitting, so that the rabbit can approach the cage door. Any sign of barking or moving toward the cage should be immediately met with a firm *"NO."* Cats, also, are not to be allowed to paw at or jump on the cage. If necessary, have someone ready to spray the cat with water. Remember to reward good behavior with generous treats.

The guinea pig is curiously checking the rabbit's grooming activity.

It is also important not to forget to talk to the animals in a friendly tone of voice.

3. Take the rabbit on your lap and allow the dog or cat to sniff it while you stroke all the animals lovingly and speak in a reassuring voice.

4. Once the animals appear to be friendly to each other, you can place the rabbit on the floor. Try this only when you feel quite sure about their behavior. Even after all adjustments have been accomplished, any free encounters should be supervised.

Caves like these, made from boards and stone, are rabbit favorites. They are cool in the summer.

Safety Outdoors

A rabbit's idea of heaven is a space to run free in the yard, nibbling on greens. Running and hopping about in the fresh air is invigorating and your rabbits will acquire a nicer looking coat. However, an unsupervised free run in the garden can turn into disaster. The animal has to be safe from other animals and weather, and from running away.

Here are some suggestions:

✔ The habitat area must include the shade of a tree or of a roof. Rabbits are extremely sensitive to heatstroke.

✔ To protect the rabbit from feline invaders, the habitat should be covered by screen or wire mesh.

✔ Rabbits dig underground tunnels and can run away. If you want to prevent escape, the floor of the habitat should be covered with wire mesh. If the run is intended to stay in the same location, the wire mesh floor can be laid below the grass level.

Can Rabbits Live Outdoors Year-Round?

Rabbits need a protective hutch for colder nights (see pages 26–27). After your rabbits are used to being outdoors and have slowly acclimated to outside temperatures, they can live in their hutch during spring, summer, and fall, or year-round in southern climates.

Hollow tree trunks are good for cover and make a great lookout seat.

Four roof tiles serve as welcome weather protection.

✔ An empty space offers neither occupation nor protection. The picture here and the one on page 54 give you some ideas about rabbit-specific habitat design.

✔ It is important to make time for petting and stroking your rabbits in their outdoor habitat. Such affection will help promote the bond between you and your pets. This way, the animals will continue to be tame and trusting outdoors as well as in the house.

Note: The ground need not be grassy. Gravel, rocks, and sand are equally adaptable to creating play and exercise areas (see photo, page 24 top). Make sure that your portable rabbit enclosure is not placed on an area that has been chemically treated.

A criblike kennel covered by screen material keeps cats out and rabbits in.

Rabbits love all kinds of natural materials (such as these from nurseries) as play spaces.

Duct pipes like these make rabbit dreams come true.

A hutch for year-round living large enough for one or two rabbits, with an additional nest box and space for food and bedding storage.

Directions:

✔ A floor space of 43 inches long, 24 inches deep, and 24 inches high (110 cm × 60 cm × 60 cm) provides for one large-breed or for two small-breed rabbits. Pine boards or a high-grade plywood can be used. We covered the interior surfaces up to approximately 6 inches (15 cm) with a non-toxic sealer to prevent erosion from urine exposure.

✔ The nest box, 16 × 16 inches (40 × 40 cm), can be removed. It is only 12 inches (30 cm) high, allowing space for the rabbit to sit on top. The entry is 6 inches (14 cm) wide and 4 inches (10 cm) above floor level.

✔ The hutch door is made from galvanized grate, 6.7 × 6.7 inches (17 × 17 cm). The right side has an additional wood lining for bad weather. Between the roof and the living quarters is a space of 7 inches (18 cm), providing air in the summer, and with storage space for bowls and other equipment.

✔ The roof is slanted toward the back in order to deflect rain. It overhangs 6 inches (14 cm) in the back, and 12 inches (30 cm) in front. It is covered with roofing paper.

✔ Underneath the hutch there is space for one bale of straw, hay, and food storage

Acclimating an Indoor Rabbit to Outdoor Living

The transition from indoor to outdoor housing has to be slow. The best time to begin this procedure is during the spring when the temperatures rise to about 64°F (18°C). By the time colder weather comes around, your rabbit will have adjusted. If the temperature drops below 59°F (15°C)

at night, the rabbit should be brought inside the house.

A Weather-Proof Hutch for Outdoor Living

I designed the hutch shown in the above photo, and an experienced breeder built it. With a little manual dexterity it can be copied at home. A shelter in the yard for a rabbit in captivity is ideal.

bags. The doors protect the rabbit from rain; the screen provides air circulation.

✔ The entire hutch is supported by four 8-inch (20-cm) two-by-fours. This and the overlapping roof serve as additional weather protection.

Supplies:

✔ Hayrack attached to left wall.

✔ Glazed stoneware food bowl.

✔ Self-watering bottle suspended through the grate. In colder weather replace the bottle daily with a bowl of tepid water.

✔ Nontoxic bedding as a bottom layer, topped with thick layers of straw.

Location:

✔ It is most suitable to place the hutch near large leafy trees to provide shade; bushes and hedges allow natural integration of hutch and environment, while offering protection from wind and rain.

✔ Try to place the hutch in a location where it will get partial sunlight so that your rabbits can benefit from the sun's warmth on cooler days, yet won't be in direct sunlight during warmer months. Also, make sure that the hutch is not exposed to harsh winds and rain in bad weather. If properly built, adequately supplied, and placed in the right setting, your hutch can provide a warm and safe shelter for your rabbits.

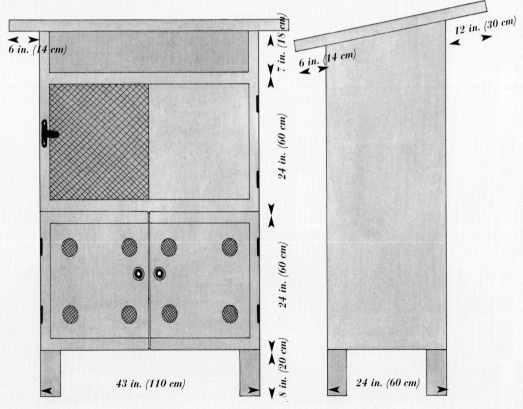

TIP

A Rabbit Playpen for Indoors

If you can't always supervise your rabbit's free-play activities, or if you just can't provide a rabbit-safe apartment, you can create a rabbit playpen. Pet stores sell a variety of models like the one shown on page 25. Make sure that it does not collapse, and protect your carpet or flooring with a plastic liner. Carpet remnants are very suitable floor materials. Provide enough exercise equipment or toys to keep the rabbit occupied (see pages 50–51). It is also important to provide a bowl of fresh water for your rabbit's playpen.

Our Abyssinian tom displays his friendship by including this rabbit in his grooming activity.

Running Free Indoors

Not everyone owns a house and garden; many rabbits are kept in apartments. No matter where, a rabbit needs to get out of its cage every day.

Allowing your rabbit to run free keeps it happy and healthy, and gives you a chance to observe its behavior.

Your rabbit's first experience to roam free outside its cage should be held off until the animal is tame and trusting. Only then can you entice it with a stem of parsley, and then gather it up and place it back into its cage. If the rabbit is still shy, it becomes extremely difficult to catch it and put it back into the cage.
Remember the following points:
✔ Always leave the cage door open to allow the rabbit to return to the nest box inside the cage for safety; this provides the sense of a private rabbit home.
✔ Place a litter pan in every room where the animal is allowed to roam free (see page 30, Housebreaking).
✔ Rabbits are quick to find their way around the house because they scent-mark their paths; however, that does not mean that you should change their run area every day. Let them discover your home slowly.

How to Prevent Accidents

Accident	Source of Danger	Prevention
Electric shock	Electrical cords and cables	Rabbits love to nibble on anything. Cover all electrical cords with duct tape or with hard tubing, or place them above the animal's reach.
Becoming crushed	Doors	Open doors slowly and carefully.
Injuries	Human feet	Watch where you walk; learn to look down.
Heatstroke	Heaters, sun	Never place the cage close to a heater or in the sun.
Poisoning	Poisonous plants	Rabbits like to chew on anything that's green; remove all plants from floor level.
Colds	Cold stone floors	Do not let rabbits run on cold stone floors; make an indoor free-run area with straw.

✔ If you cannot keep a constant eye on your rabbit during its indoor free run, you can set up an enclosed space within a room. But remember that it won't be happy hopping around in wide-open areas over bare floors. Your rabbit will prefer to crawl under chests of drawers, behind closets and couches, and even to hop along the wall. A play area suitable for the natural capacities of your rabbit will provide variety for your pet and be fun for you to watch.

✔ Little playhouses can be made out of cardboard boxes; cut windows in them for the rabbit to slip in and out of. Make sure that the top of the box is stable enough to bear the rabbit's weight when it jumps up on it. Wood and plastic playhouses are also available at the pet shop.

✔ Young animals may be too small to get out of the deep cage pan. To help them, place a piece of wood inside and outside the cage door. Placing a small piece of carpet over the door grid will prevent their little feet from sustaining injuries.

✔ Check the whereabouts of your little friend while it is roaming around. Is it nibbling at the leg of your favorite chair? A clear "No," and a loud clap of your hands will teach it to stop. Try not to frighten the animal but be firm and persistant in reprimanding your rabbit. A rabbit reacts to your voice and you can influence its behavior, all depending on whether you talk loud or soft to it, use a coaxing or more severe tone of voice.

✔ Watch out where you walk. Rabbits are masters at sudden jumps across your path.

RABBITS AND VACATIONS

Rabbits are not suitable for vacation travel because they suffer from changes in climate and environment.

Home Care: Your rabbit is most comfortable at home. Find a reliable pet sitter long before you leave for vacation. Give detailed instructions, in writing, and leave your phone number and a veterinarian's address.

Pet Boarding: You can board your rabbit in a pet sitter's home or in a pet motel. Get references from your pet store or breeder, and check out the place personally.

Taking the Rabbit Abroad: Foreign travel requires special health certification. Get information early. Most traveling is very stressful for rabbits. A hutch in a vacation home would be the best solution.

If you do travel with the rabbit, the transport container must be safe and water must be available throughout the trip. If you travel by car take frequent breaks and calm the animal.

Housebreaking

Rabbits are clean animals by nature and this can work to your advantage. You will notice that your rabbit deposits its excreta mainly in one corner of the cage. Wild rabbits keep their underground burrows clean by using certain areas for their fecal deposits. When you let your rabbit run free in the house, it will soon display this same behavior and you can use this to plan the right placement of the litter box. Rabbits do not cover their excrement as cats do because they leave their feces as scent "messages." Rabbits also defecate a lot more often than cats do, which makes it harder for them to hop into a litter box every time. However, with a little patience, you can train your rabbit to use a litter box. Toilet training should begin in the cage.

The Litter Box

Pet stores sell litter boxes in a variety of sizes and materials. Models for kittens are suitable for small bunnies. You can use this type of pan for the indoor cage. Put the box filled with kitty litter into the cage corner where your rabbit likes to deposit its feces and urine. Once the rabbit is accustomed to going in there, it will use this toilet even when it has its first free run in your home. If the free runs get longer, you might want to set up a second toilet.

✔ A larger litter box is more suitable for the floor while your rabbit has the free run of the house. This pan should be large enough for the animal to dig, play, and roll around in.

✔ Special hard resin boards are available for placement underneath the litter, which enables your rabbit to keep its nails short while scratching and digging.

✔ Remember, the smaller litter box goes inside the cage where most of the fecal pellets are deposited.

This tame Dalmatian Rex enjoys being hand-fed by his little friend.

✔ Leave the cage door open during the first free-roaming experience. Many rabbits go back to their cage box to relieve themselves.

✔ The second litter box is placed in the area where the rabbit is most likely to sit or play.

✔ Add some of the litter and fecal pellets from the cage litter box to scent-mark the box in the room.

✔ From time to time, pick up the rabbit and place it in the box. Keep putting your rabbit into the box in the room; don't lose patience if it hops out and relieves itself somewhere else. Eventually your rabbit will get accustomed to using its second toilet. Sometimes a rabbit learns faster if you allow short but frequent outings. Hold off feeding greens until the evening or until after the last outing.

✔ Fecal pellets are easily swept up or vacuumed; urine stains are best removed with the same agents that are sold in pet stores as cat urine neutralizers, or you can clean up urine puddles with vinegar and water. Never punish a rabbit for its being "dirty"; you will only destroy any confidence that you have already established.

HOW-TO: GROOMING

The Well-Maintained Cage

A clean cage is an important part of disease prevention.

Daily: Aerate the straw bedding and wash the food bowl with hot water. The water bottle must be scrubbed twice weekly. Get spare bottles and sipper tubes, and soak them overnight in water with a few drops of bleach. Rinse thoroughly.

Weekly: Replace the entire bedding. Straw and shavings can be composted. Cat litter goes into the trash. The litter pan must be washed with hot water, and the scale is best removed with the addition of citric acid from the pet store.

Monthly: Wash the top grate thoroughly with hot water.

Fur Care for Shorthaired and Normal-Hair Breeds

Outdoor rabbits need to be brushed only during the fall and spring when they change their coat. Indoor rabbits shed year-round, and need to be brushed weekly, preferably with a natural bristle brush.

Caring for Longhaired Coats

Foxes are combed weekly with a metal comb or with a special brush that has angled wire bristles. Jamoras and Angoras are best groomed daily because their fine wool tends to mat. Matted hair must be cut away with scissors. These animals also must be shorn or clipped every three months. Ask an experienced person to show you how this is done.

How to Pick Up a Rabbit

Small breeds and pups are picked up by gently holding them between two hands.

✔ All other animals are firmly grasped by the scruff of the neck behind the ears, while the other hand supports the hindquarters.

✔ To carry the rabbit, place it on your left forearm, while you continue stabilizing the body with your right hand.

Note: Large and heavy rabbits are better supported by holding them against your chest, keeping a light but firm grasp on their scruff. Children can carry rabbits best in a basket. One hand should always be held close to the animal to prevent injuries from an unexpected jump.

One hand holds the loose fur on the back, the other hand supports the rear and legs.

Nail Clipping

As soon as the nails begin to curve downward they must be clipped. You need to use a special nail clipper to avoid splitting the nails.

If you have never done this procedure, I recommend that you have someone show you how to do it. A veterinarian's assistant, the breeder, or a pet store helper can best assist you.
How-to:

✔ Place the animal on your lap or on a slip-proof surface. Hold the paw between thumb and index finger, and push the fur just lightly back while exerting gentle pressure to allow the nail to protrude.

✔ Inside each nail is a channel that contains blood vessels and nerves. Cut the nail at an angle to about 1/8 inch (0.5 cm) above this visible channel.

Rabbits can be carried like this when they are too big to fit in the curve of a child's arm.

Nails have to be cut with a special nail clipper. The inset shows the cutting angle.

Dental check. This is the correct dental alignment. The upper incisors overlap the lower.

✔ If you cause a nail to bleed, press a small cotton pad on the nail to stop the bleeding. A little wound spray aids in protecting this minor injury.

✔ When you need to clip dark-colored nails, hold the nail over a flashlight in order to see the blood vessel.

Dental Checkup

Rabbit teeth grow continually. Daily rations of greens help keep teeth at the right length. Inherited malocclusion prevents normal abrasion. These teeth have to be trimmed regularly by a veterinarian.

Rabbits are herbivores. Youngsters must be adapted slowly to plants and branches.

The Proper Nutrition

The diet of wild rabbits consists almost exclusively of fresh plants. In arid areas and during winter months, dry plants, bark, and branches make up the rabbits' meal.

Rabbits need a high-fiber diet to regulate digestion. Too much grain makes the animal fat, and does not agree with its natural requirements. Correct nutrition is essential.

Commercial Dry Foods

Pet stores offer a variety of commercial foods in pellet form.

✔ Young animals should be fed specific growth formulas.

Remember the following:

✔ Do not buy outdated food. Vitamins and other nutrients are destroyed with time. The packages are dated.

✔ You are better off buying packaged pellets than the less expensive loose bulk because only the packaged foods guarantee the correct nutrient composition.

✔ Certified pellets combined with lots of fresh greens make up an optimal meal plan.

Note: Some rabbits will try to eat selectively, choosing the more fattening foods from the meal assortment. If your rabbit is as clever as that, be persistent—do not replenish the food until everything is eaten, or you can change to pellets exclusively for a while. Pellets contain everything the animal needs, from greens to grains.

Daily Hay

Hay is the staple food in a rabbit's daily diet, as bread is for us. High-quality hay is an essential and irreplaceable part of each day's meal. The hay rack should never be empty. Hay is not fattening, and it regulates the digestive process. If you notice that one of your rabbits is becoming too fat, place it on a hay-and-water diet one day a week.

You can recognize *high-quality* hay by its light green color and its aromatic smell. It contains herbs, flowers, and a variety of grasses.

Low-grade hay is quite dusty looking; its color is pale yellowish, and it contains mainly one type of grass.

Be very careful not to feed hay that is spoiled or moldy; it causes serious illness.

Highly recommended is hay from mountain meadows and from untreated organic fields.

Golden Rules
on Food and Maintenance

1 Feeding should take place on a regular schedule, preferably twice a day: Morning: dry food; Evening: greens and other fresh foods.

2 Sufficient hay and fresh water should always be available.

3 Food should be richly varied all year.

4 Never change food drastically or suddenly. Youngsters must be allowed to adjust slowly to greens by being given them only in very gradually increasing amounts.

5 Never use food directly from the refrigerator or freezer, and avoid canned foods.

6 Never offer food that is chemically treated, spoiled, or moldy.

7 Approach the rabbit slowly, while talking in a calm voice. Bend or kneel and allow the animal to smell your hand, then lift it into your arms.

8 Rabbits love to be gently scratched on the scruff of the neck and stroked all over their body. They do not enjoy being scratched by fingertips either under the chin or along the belly.

9 If you allow your rabbits to run free every day they will reward you with good health and happiness.

10 Keep indoor and outdoor cages meticulously clean to prevent illness.

Water

There are still some people who think that rabbits do not need fresh water if they eat greens. That is not true, although water consumption varies individually. Some of my rabbits drink 1 pint (400 ml) every day!

Make sure that the water bottle is always filled with fresh water. When you have very young animals you need to check the water level to be sure that they are drinking. It may be necessary to teach them to drink from the bottle by leading them to it and gently activating the water flow.

Note: Use dilute chamomile tea to treat bouts of enteric problems. Rabbits will gladly drink this.

Greens and Fresh Foods

Today's manufactured rabbit foods contain all the ingredients of healthful rabbit nutrition. This kind of food is easy to use, does not spoil quickly, and is easy to obtain. However, fresh foods are not only a natural choice (a rabbit's digestive system is designed for eating plants and its teeth are best worn down by nibbling on green foods and branches), but they are also more flavorful. Nutritional components and vita-

mins are natural and unaltered only in fresh foods. These foods offer variety in addition to dry pellets, they enhance an otherwise monotonous meal plan, and they keep your pets happy and healthy.

Meals from Kitchen and Garden

The favorite foods of your little furry gourmets are: Vitamin-rich parsley, field salad greens, carrots with greens, and all fruits, with apples ranking at the top.

Gardeners may want to grow a variety of roots and herbs to have highly nutritious and flavorful foods ready for their rabbits.

Other suitable fresh foods are fennel, celery, kohlrabi, chicory, the leaves of horseradish, radishes, broccoli, and spinach, and the greens of beans and soybeans. Herbs such as dill, parsley, and sage are also suitable, as well as the leaves and stems of raspberries (two or three fruits may be given as treats).

Rabbits and guinea pigs love the same treats.

A Meal Plan to Keep Your Rabbit Fit and Healthy

Mornings	Daily ration of pellets: Dwarf rabbits: 1 ounce (30g; 3 tablespoons); Small breeds: 1.8 ounces (50g; 5 tablespoons); Young rabbits: (for four months) growth formula pellets
Evenings	Greens (dandelion greens, carrot greens, corn salad): Dwarf rabbits: a small handful; Small breeds: two handfuls; Young rabbits: add greens gradually, as little as one or two leaves of parsley or dandelion
	Alternating with greens: Dwarf rabbits: One carrot, or 1/2 fennel root Small and large breeds: approximately double portions
Also Daily	Hopper full of hay; bottle filled with fresh water
Once Weekly	Two to three branches, alternating with one small piece of hard whole-wheat grain bread, or one wholewheat grain cracker
Every Other Week	Treats: healthy chew sticks such as unsprayed twigs

Cabbage is only *moderately healthful* because it causes bloating, as does lettuce, unless organic, because it is usually chemically treated.

Do not feed tomatoes, zucchini, eggplant, beets, raw potatoes, and cucumbers. Potato sprouts and uncooked beans are *poisonous.*

Wild Plants

Find greens in undeveloped meadows, fields, and off-road paths lined by wild plants. Do not pick greens along traveled roads, where dogs relieve themselves, and where agricultural pesticides are sprayed.

If you don't know how to choose wild plants and herbs there are a number of easy plant identification guides available in your library or bookstore.

Rabbit favorites are: dandelions, meadow grass, ribwort, broad-leaved plantain, vetch, hogweed, goosefoot, and coltsfoot. Also, the

young leaves of wild strawberries and raspberries, blackberries, nettles, and chamomile.

Harmful or poisonous are: potato sprouts, raw beans, foxglove, crocus, yew tree, hemlock, wild poppies, creeping buttercup, lobelia and toadflax, milkweed, and goldenrod.

Foods to Chew

Rabbits love to chew, and chewing foods keeps the ever-growing teeth at the right length. *Throughout the entire year* rabbits need to chew on twigs with buds and leaves: pussy willow, beech, alder, linden, maple, ash, and fruit trees (organically grown only, never frozen!), and from time to time, a piece of hard wholegrain bread or crackers (without spices). From the many available chew sticks in your pet store try to choose the products that contain more greens and vegetables than grains.

The Subject of Offspring

Rabbits have many natural predators. The species has survived because rabbits mature early and reproduce abundantly.

If you decide to get a pair of rabbits and want to avoid unwanted offspring, it is essential that you make sure the siblings are of the same sex. If they are not, the buck must be neutered as soon as possible (page 10).
Note: Please do not mate rabbits "for the fun of it." The pups are very cute but, except for some dwarf breeds, most have very little chance of finding a responsible home.

The Pregnant Doe

Once the doe is pregnant, intended or not, you have to treat the animal appropriately. Make preparations for a healthy pregnancy and healthy offspring.

Important information and advice:

✔ Count 31 days from mating to birth (after 33 days veterinary assistance is required).

✔ Mother and pups must have their own quarters through the pregnancy until the pups are weaned.

✔ Don't be surprised if you notice behavioral changes in the doe. Some normally tense females become more amiable, while others may display unusual sensitivities.

✔ During the second half of the pregnancy, the doe should be picked up as little as possible. Never try to pick up a pregnant doe by holding her under the belly. This would endanger the unborn pups.

✔ One week before the delivery it is important to clean and disinfect the cage and everything in it.

✔ Place a nest box inside the doe's cage. It is of the same size as the regular "house" but this one must have a floor that enables you to remove the box, the nest, and the pups all at once. The top of the box should be hinged or removable for easy inspection of the litter. Does usually accept the box gratefully, and proceed by lining it with straw.

✔ One or several days before she gives birth, the doe begins to pull the fur from her belly area to line her nest.

At five weeks it's easy to sit up for a treat.

Birth and Nest Patrol

Rabbits give birth quickly and silently, and you should try to not disturb the doe. A few hours after the birth you need to lift the doe gently out of the cage, remove the top of the nest box, and check the health and condition of the newborn pups by carefully looking underneath the furry blanket. Remove any dead pups, and any remainders of the after-birth.

Note: If you notice a pup outside of the fur-lined nest, immediately place it among the warmth of its littermates; left unchecked, the pup would get cold and die. Unlike a cat, a rabbit doe will not replace such offspring in the nest.

Adorable as they may be, at five weeks rabbit pups must still stay with Mom.

The Young Rabbit

Rabbits are born nest-bound, blind, deaf, and naked. The doe will nurse them once or twice daily, and they gain weight quickly during the ensuing several weeks. At about three weeks the first of the litter begins to move around and start nibbling on straw and foods. This is the time to offer special growth feed to the pups. Pet stores sell the appropriate diets for all growth stages of your rabbits. At the age of seven weeks the pups may be placed in their new homes.

BEHAVIOR AND ACTIVITIES

It is as much fun to observe rabbits as it is to get an insight into the behavior of these little survival artists. Learning to understand your rabbits will make your interactions a truly joyful experience.

Body Language

Rabbits display a variety of types of body language.

Sitting up: "What's going on over there?"

Sudden ducking: The animal presses its entire body flat against the floor, remaining motionless with ears lying flat. This behavior stems from the wild rabbit's expression of fear of predators. It always means "I am scared."

Ducking when you approach: This behavior indicates submission. The animal wants to appease you.

Sitting calmly, ears aligned with the back: The rabbit is resting.

Lying on its side, belly exposed, ears erect: The rabbit is recovering from running or from exposure to heat. It is relaxing.

Same as above but with ears lying flat: Total relaxation.

Torso stretched out forward, ears erect, hind legs posed for a sudden jump: Tense posture toward someone new or unfamiliar: The animal may move forward carefully, sniff, yet remain ready to jump. Insecurity prevails when the little cottontail is folded downward. Tail folded upward signals increased trust and security.

Watch out when you see a rabbit that stretches its head aggressively forward, ears flatly aligned toward the back. Contrary to the submissive posture previously described, in this posture the rabbit's hind legs are supported, ready to jump for a quick and sudden attack. If you do not understand this warning you may suffer serious bites or scratches.

Note: Some rabbits are so protective of their cage area that they paw aggressively even at their own keeper's hands when they reach inside the cage. There is only one remedy: with patience and calming talk, place your hand flat, from above, over the top of the animal's head. This will instantly produce a calming effect. When I took care of an aggressive doe in my house I had occasion to try this method repeatedly, and it worked reliably every time.

Sitting up is a natural pose for all breeds of rabbits.

The Language of Scents

Rabbits have a highly refined sense of smell, much better than that of humans. They communicate by leaving each other scent messages. A variety of glands produce the necessary scents. If rabbits are unfamiliar with each other they first sniff each other's nose; then the anal scents are carefully checked out.

A Dalmatian Rex doe is a little pushy in getting the dwarf buck's attention while he is engrossed in his grooming.

The *anal glands* are located on either side of the vent. Rabbits use anal secretions to cover their fecal matter, which is used to mark their territory.

Once acquainted, the new friends gently touch their faces together.

Scent glands are also located inside the hairless folds of the genital orifice. These glands produce a somewhat sweet, pungent scent, which is quite strong. Rabbits leave their scent like business cards that tell the next animal whether they belong to the same family, which sex they are, and when a doe is ready to mate.

While the *chin glands* are actually located underneath the tongue, they secrete their scent on the surface of the skin underneath the chin. Humans are unable to identify this scent, which marks a chosen mate as well as the rabbit's territory. To mark their objects, such as the legs of

chairs, the corners of a cage, their nest box, branches, and so on, notice how rabbits rub the objects with the underside of their chin.

Rabbits do not feel secure when they enter another's territory; rightly so, because in the wild they would quickly be driven out by the owners. For this reason it is important to allow unfamiliar rabbits to meet in a neutral area, and place them in the same cage only after they are well acquainted (see page 19).

These two strangers sniff each other's nose at first.

UNDERSTANDING
TYPES OF BEHAVIOR

If you want to communicate with your rabbits you need to understand their language.

 This is what your rabbit is doing.

 What is my rabbit trying to say?

 This is how you should react.

 The rabbit is digging.

 Wild rabbits dig their holes in the groun

 Fence the rabbit's outdoor area securely; a sandbox to the indoor cage for digging.

 All fours are stretched out.
 Relaxed posture, resting.
 This rabbit wants to be left alone.

This Dwarf Lop is busily grooming itself.
Rabbits keep their fur meticulously clean.
This is essential behavior in order to maintain a dry coat. Avoid moisture in the straw bedding.

 This rabbit is yawning.

 It is tired from running and playing.

 Give it a well-deserved rest.

👆 These two Ermine rabbits are pressing their heads together.

❓ They are friends.

❗ Rabbits need physical contact.

👆 These two are circling each other.

❓ The buck is trying to mount the doe.

❗ If she is in heat she will be pregnant in no time.

This Belgian hare is 👆 sitting up.

This behavior indicates surveillance. ❓

The cage must be high enough ❗ for the animals to sit up straight.

A rabbit running at full speed. 👆

Rabbits are extremely fast and agile. ❓

Never chase a running rabbit: it is likely to ❗ react with panic.

👆 This buck is rubbing his chin against the broomstick.

❓ He is marking his territory with his chin glands.

❗ Rabbits feel safe and content only if they have marked the area they inhabit.

TIP

How to Deal with Shy Rabbits

If, after a normal period of adjustment, your rabbit remains shy or fearful, it is usually due to a genetic predisposition or improper care and handling.

Here are some helpful tips:

✔ If the rabbit consistently escapes into its box, you need to remove the box for a while.

✔ Place the cage in a higher location to allow the rabbit a better point of surveillance.

✔ Withhold the daily free-roaming period for a while; chasing after the rabbit to catch it may be causing it too much panic.

✔ Approach the cage slowly and speak in a calm voice, then offer a treat through the cage bars.

✔ As often as possible place the animal on your lap and gently stroke and cuddle it.

If the Rabbit Is Too Quiet

Wild rabbits have many predators: badgers, foxes, and birds of prey, as well as cats and dogs. Above all, however, humans are their worst enemy, wiping out entire colonies with guns, poisons, or other "pest-destruction" methods because they consider rabbits to be a nuisance.

Wild rabbits must behave extremely quietly and unobtrusively in order to avoid being discovered by predators. Although every rabbit develops its own individual personality, it nevertheless possesses innate behavior traits that it shares with all rabbits. Your rabbit won't feel safe and trusting with you until you've learned the animal's natural behavior patterns and take them into consideration in your day-to-day dealings with it. Our pet rabbits retain the trait of communicating with scent and body language rather than with sounds. In certain circumstances, however, even rabbits emit sounds that humans can clearly understand.

Grunting: These are quick sequences of sounds that indicate annoyance. This is the way your rabbit voices complaints when you place it back into its cage earlier than it wanted.

Screaming: When grabbed unexpectedly, a shy and fearful rabbit screams in panic. If this happens, quickly wrap the animal in a little blanket and place it back in its cage. Panic-stricken rabbits can die of shock (see page 58).

Growling ("Purring"): This sound is usually heard from bucks after the mating act.

Dogs and rabbits may well be best friends, but they should not be left together unsupervised.

Sensory Capabilities of Rabbits

Nose: Nares are highly flexible and contain one million olfactory cells.	Excellent scent perception; communicate by scent-marking.
Ears: Formed like sound funnels, they can be moved individually; hearing range extends to 360 degrees.	Excellent hearing ability; react with fear and panic to unfamiliar loud noises; recognize humans by voice.
Eyes: Located relatively high and more laterally than forward; pupils can be minimally narrowed. View range overlaps only minimally. Sight is focused on distance.	Able to see an entire view circle, which is important to escape predators. Bright lights have blinding effect. See objects two-dimensionally rather than three-dimensionally as humans do. Poor sight for near objects.
Sensory Hairs: These hairs are as long as the body is wide.	Hairs enable the animal to find entry into burrows in the dark.
Taste Buds: Found in the mucosal surfaces of the mouth and throat.	Enable rabbits to differentiate sweet, sour, bitter, and salty. Domesticated rabbits can no longer differentiate poisonous plants reliably.

Squeaking: Sound of young pups expressing cold or hunger.

Hissing growl: Expresses defense and aggression. A quick attack may follow.

Grinding teeth: Always expresses pain. The sick or injured rabbit displays apathy and looks weak and dull.

Quiet churning sounds produced by the jaws: Expresses well-being; accompanies cuddles and petting.

Drumming: The rabbit vehemently stamps the floor with its hind legs. It expresses excitement and irritation. Wild rabbits use this to alert their neighbors of approaching predators.

Grooming and Social Interaction

Rabbits groom themselves regularly and thoroughly several times daily. *Licking* keeps the fur clean and smooth. This is essential to keep the animal healthy and to keep the body temperature even.

During the shedding season, however, you should make a habit of brushing your rabbit to remove old, dead hairs. For rabbits that are kept in the home, the shedding season can last for several months. Brushing also acts as a massage, promoting better blood circulation to the skin and allowing new hairs to grow more quickly.

A most adorable sight is a rabbit sitting on its hindquarters, washing its little face. To do so it licks its paws to wet them, and then rubs its ears and eyes in a circular motion; then it "combs" its hair by nibbling inch by inch along its furry body. The nails of the hind paws take care of an itchy spot on the head.

As part of the cleaning routine, wild rabbits also roll in warm sand, which helps with parasite removal. My pet rabbits enjoy themselves by rolling in their litter pan of granulated clay (see page 30). In addition, our sociable rabbits practice interactive body care (see photo, page 49). While they rest, rabbits lie close to each other, licking each other's head and ears. This is not so much a behavior of cleanliness as an expression of friendship and trust within the extended family. This is the reason why you need to pet your rabbit regularly to reinforce the human-animal bond.

How to pet your rabbit: With the tips of your fingers stroke the animal's nose upward to the forehead. This is a calming gesture. Stroke the animal along the back with your flat hand. Gently take the ears between two fingers and stroke them from the root to the tip. Gentle scratching behind the ears and neck may give rise to the sound of churning jaws, an expression of true delight. This sound must not be mistaken for the gnashing of teeth, which expresses pain (see page 47).

Group housing gives us insight into many types of rabbit behavior.

Never tug at the sensitive tactile hairs (located on both sides of the mouth-nose area, above the eyes, and on the cheeks) or worse, cut them off. Without them your rabbit would be deprived of an important tool that it uses for orientation. The skin all over the rabbit's body is capable of registering contact stimuli. This is

Despite its love for active play, rabbits need time to rest and relax.

Mutual grooming reinforces group bonding.

why it relaxes them and they thoroughly enjoy it when they can huddle in a corner of their home or when you reassuringly run your hand over their coat. My rabbits particularly like it when I run my finger from the starting point of the root of the nose upward to the forehead. **Note:** Never, not even in play, scratch your rabbit under the chin or along its belly. The rabbit interprets this as torture, and it will react with flight or attack. This is one sure way of creating aggressive rabbits!

How your rabbit helps you stay clean: Since grooming is a social behavior, your rabbit will include you in its "fur care" by either licking your hand or arm, or even your sweater. It means "I like you" if your rabbit licks your hand or your clothing in an excess of enthusiasm. When I pet my rabbit, he responds not only with licking but also with gentle nibbles that make small holes in my T-shirts.
Note: When you stop petting, your pet may respond by scratching with its front paws. This means "Please don't stop." The same message may be expressed by pushing your hand with its mouth. If your rabbit pushes your hand vehemently aside, however, you need to leave it alone immediately; this rabbit can bite you if you insist on overcoming the rejection.

Learning to Sit Up

This exercise trains the rabbit in its natural behavior of stretching upward to survey its habitat.

Try these exercises:

✔ Hold a treat in front of the rabbit at floor level.
✔ As soon as the rabbit starts nibbling, lift the food slightly.
✔ Offer the next treat at a higher level to encourage stretching.
✔ Practice this before mealtime because a hungry rabbit is more motivated to reach up.

Stretching high for a treat keeps the body fit.

While one little rascal is hiding, the other is jumping across the hideout.

The more fit and agile your rabbits are, the more they will delight in this play.

Fitness Training for Fun

Rabbits are very agile and are natural jumpers. The smallest breeds are the most amazing acrobats, while the larger breeds are slower and less mobile despite their longer legs.

✔ No matter which breed, however, they all love to jump hurdles.
✔ Place obstacles along the wall, and make sure they are long enough not to encourage the rabbit to run around them.
✔ The height should be level with the animal's height when sitting; the width should not exceed the length of the rabbit.
✔ Obstacles can be homemade from wood, or you can use bricks, stones, or cans of various sizes.
✔ Entice the rabbit to play by offering treats. Most rabbits love this play and jump the obstacles without encouragement.

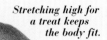

This "nibble tree" grows only healthy treats.

The Nibble Tree

This tree offers exercise to bored and lazy indoor rabbits.

✔ The floor board is made from high-grade plywood, approximately 16 inches (40 cm) in diameter.

✔ On top of the board attach a piece of wood approximately 15 inches (35 cm) high, 3 inches (8 cm) thick.

✔ Drill holes of varying sizes in the wood.

✔ Place treats inside the holes, such as carrots, twigs, apple slices, or herbs.

✔ You can make the tree available every time the rabbits have their free-running period.

Playland for Rabbits

While the animals are running free they still need to be occupied with games that further their natural behavior. This is particularly true if you only have one rabbit. Either place a variety of cartons with access holes in the play area, or you can buy ready-made playhouses in pet stores. The curious rabbit will love to discover the openings, and jump on the roof. A wooden box containing lots of paper towels or toilet tissue makes a great place for burrowing and cuddling. Rabbits love a well-supplied, deep litter box for digging and rolling around with delight. Bricks and boards are also creative places. Make sure that all play areas are secure and strong enough to support the weight of your rabbits. Wobbly paths make shy rabbits more insecure.

Keep Exercise Moderate!
While small tricks, such as sitting up, need practice, you need to proceed slowly with the exercises; otherwise, you could turn play into stress.

Treats are great motivators.

Rabbits feel protected in this wood house and love to climb on its roof.

PREVENTIVE HEALTH CARE AND ILLNESS

Rabbits are naturally resistant to illness. Many illnesses are caused by incorrect maintenance and nutrition, so watch your pet closely. The earlier a symptom is recognized, the better are the chances of healing.

Prevention Is Better than Cure

When you bring a new rabbit to an already-existing group it is essential that you keep the newcomer in a separate cage for at least two to three weeks. This protects your pets from an infection that was not evident at the time of purchase. Also, the stress of moving to a new home may bring an existing illness to the surface. Vaccination is another protective measure (see pages 54–55).

Nutritional mistakes that can lead to illness:
✔ Sudden changes in foods
✔ Spoiled foods
✔ Too much or too little food
✔ Lack of fresh water

Maintenance mistakes that can lead to illness:
✔ Drafts
✔ Dampness (lack of shelter outdoors)
✔ Sudden changes in temperature
✔ Heat and indoor heating that is too dry (heat kills more rabbits than diseases do!)
✔ Stress from noise and commotion
✔ Unsanitary cage conditions
✔ Lack of nurturing care

First Warning Signs

The earlier a disease is recognized and treated, the higher are the chances of a cure.
1. Observe your rabbit's behavioral patterns closely, especially during feeding and playtimes.
2. Take written notes of any changes. These records may be critical for a veterinary evaluation at a later date.

Symptoms of disease:
✔ The rabbit does not come at its usual pace to greet you at mealtime.
✔ The animal is eating less or not at all.
✔ The rabbit appears apathetic or does not come out of its nest box.
✔ The rabbit shows no interest in play; it remains listless in the cage.
✔ Severe pain can be recognized by a quiet sound of grinding teeth and a blank stare. Be careful not to miss this very low sound because of surrounding noises.
Note: Page 55 lists more symptoms of diseases.

This rabbit has chosen a flowerpot as a hiding place.

When Your Rabbit Is Ill

Even the best-kept rabbits can get sick. Novices should seek the advice of experienced breeders, and in case of doubt or obvious pain or discomfort, you must take the rabbit to the nearest animal clinic. Once you have established contact with breeders and clubs, you need to get current information on the prevalence of infectious diseases in your geographical region. Be especially aware of a viral disease called *Myxomatosis.* The myxoma virus is transmitted by blood-sucking insects such as fleas and mosquitoes. *Acute symptoms* of the disease include swollen eyelids, followed by a discharge and swelling of the head and genital area. The head becomes deformed and swollen bumps

Bricks and roof tiles make a cozy place to snuggle.

form all over the body. Death follows as a result of exhaustion.

Preventive measures:

✔ Insect control and installation of screens on outdoor cages.

✔ Avoid greens from areas that are habitats for wild rabbits.

✔ Vaccination is available at the age of six weeks; it protects the animal for six to nine months.

Some other common health problems in rabbits are:

Snuffles: This respiratory disease is caused by one or both of the bacteria Pasteurella and Bordetella. Symptoms are sneezing, nasal discharge, or a tilted head. The latter means that the inner ear is infected. This disease must be treated by a veterinarian as early as possible in order to control the bacteria and to prevent spreading the disease.

Sore hocks: The feet and pads are sensitive to moisture from urine, which may lead to sore, swollen, and finally abscessed areas. Young males are often actively stamping their feet, making them even more susceptible. The best prevention are lots of dry straw and dry sitting boards. Sore hocks must be thoroughly cleansed, dried, and medicated.

Enteritis complex: A combination of bacterial enteric pathogens and a condition of lowered immune resistance may lead to diarrhea or constipation, and mucoid discharge from the intestines. The rabbit may or may not stop eating. Instead of the usual small fecal balls, the vent appears wet and caked and the excreted material may be colorless, covered with whitish mucus. Give the sick rabbit hay cubes and yogurt. Many rabbits have a sweet tooth, and they will gladly take a strawberry-flavored yogurt, which helps to reestablish the intestinal flora. If the condition does not improve within two days, veterinary treatment is recommended.

Ear mites: Treat the ears of your rabbits monthly with a few drops of ear mite medication to prevent painful ear infections. Keep the ears meticulously clean, without a trace of dark deposits.

Reminder: The most important preventions of disease are cleanliness and good nutrition. This includes ample layers of straw and generous supplies of clean, absorbable nontoxic bedding. Tender loving care and close observation add the final touches to a healthful plan for life.

Checklist
Signs of Disease

1 Fur: Appears dull; no longer lies flat and smooth.

2 Eyes: Have lost their alert clarity; now appear dull and blank.

3 Fecal excreta: Have lost their healthy, round, and firm consistency; may become thick and unformed, or there may be watery, thin diarrhea, foul-smelling or mixed with blood. Emergency veterinary treatment is required immediately.

4 Urine: Color of urine in rabbits changes according to their food intake. It can vary from light yellow to red-brown.

5 Body temperature: Normal is 101.3–103.1°F (38.5–39.5°C). Higher as well as lower temperatures are symptoms of illness.

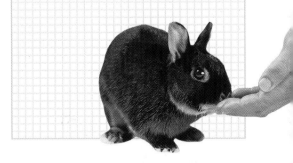

Visiting a Veterinary Clinic

Choose a veterinarian who specializes in exotic animals, which includes rabbits. Your pet store can help you find the right veterinarian. Take your rabbit in a strong, preferably plastic-lined, transport box. Write down all necessary information: age, sex, source, how long you have owned the rabbit, and what kind of changes you noticed first and when. Also, write down what you feed the animal, and take along a fecal sample.

Don't hesitate to ask the veterinarian questions about how to treat your rabbit. Ask to be shown how to perform any necessary procedures.

Minor Health Problems

Most of the time, if a rabbit is feeling poorly it is a diet-related problem. In many cases, such problems can be cleared up by medications that can be found in your home medicine chest. The following is a list of symptoms of minor problems and what you can do to remedy them.

Mild diarrhea: The rabbit appears to be in good spirits but the anal area is soiled with soft fecal matter.

Treatment: Stop all greens and fresh foods immediately and replace the water with dilute chamomile tea; feed only hay. Clean and disinfect the cage and replace the bedding to create a dry and warm place. Hang a salt spool in the

cage to enhance mineral intake. If the condition persists after two days, take the animal and a fecal sample to the veterinarian.

Constipation: As opposed to diarrhea, this problem is only noticed when the rabbit stops eating and becomes listless and if you notice the animal hunched up in the back of the cage, trying to expel a few hard and dry fecal pellets. Check the litter box as well.

Treatment: First check whether the water bottle is blocked, preventing the rabbit from drinking. Remove all dry foods, and replace them with only fresh greens such as parsley and carrot greens. Let the rabbit run free. For immediate care, administer 1 teaspoon of linseed and paraffin oil three times daily. Gently massage the belly of the animal, moving your fingers in a circular motion. Seek veterinary help if no change is evident after 24 hours. **Note:** If you think that the constipation may have existed for some time, or if the rabbit appears bloated, you should take it to a veterinarian immediately.

The coat must be kept clean and dry to protect your rabbit from cold and dampness.

Emergency First Aid

In some situations only swift attention will save your rabbit's life. You must be ready to provide first aid and be prepared to take appropriate action.

Heatstroke: Rabbits do not tolerate heat well. Most frequently, accidents occur in the summer when you place the rabbit cage outside and forget that the sun moves—suddenly the animal is exposed to the sun without a place to hide. The same danger of heatstroke exists when the rabbit has to ride or sit in a car without air conditioning.

Regular outdoor activities condition the rabbit and increase its resistance to diseases.

Symptoms of heatstroke: You find the rabbit lying flat on the ground, barely breathing, the body trembling; the nares are wide open, and the mucosals appear bluish.

First aid: As quickly as possible place the animal in a cool area, preferably indoors. If you are on the road, get into the shade as quickly as possible or try to reach a rest area.

To lower the body temperature, place the animal on your lap and wrap it in a cold or cool wet towel. Do not use ice. Repeat the wrap each time the towel starts to feel warm. To stimulate the circulation, give the patient some coffee: large breeds, 1 tablespoon; dwarf rabbits, 1 teaspoon; small breeds, 1 to 2 teaspoons. When the animal begins to recover, leave it in the cool area, allow it to move around, and encourage it to drink fresh water.

Shock from panicking: Tense and shy rabbits are most affected. They may panic in fear, feel trapped or surprised, and will suffer a shock, which can lead to death. This shock can be caused simply by the noise of an overhead airplane while the rabbit is in the yard, or by the sudden sound of a vacuum cleaner. Rabbits also get panicky and can suffer from anxiety attacks when chased by a dog or cat. The affected rabbit tries to flee, finds no escape, and ends up pressing its body flat against the floor, ears laid back in a breathless state of fear.

Symptoms: You find the rabbit flat and motionless on the ground, body trembling, pupils rigid and dilated. Some rabbits let out one or several deathly screams when they are mortally afraid. Even when the immediate danger has passed, a delayed shock reaction may occur. The rabbit will then lie there impassively, the pupils of the eyes wide open, the eyes bulging as if about to pop out of its head, and its little body will tremble uncontrollably.

First aid: Approach the animal slowly and speak in a soothing voice. Grab it quickly and firmly by the neck and, supporting the back, place the animal as quickly as possible in a darkened transport box, where it will feel safe and hidden. If the animal screams in fear, wrap it in a blanket as you pick it up. If a blanket is not available, use any piece of clothing to create a dark wrap as quickly as possible, and hold it in your arm or lap. Keep the rabbit warm and make sure it gets absolute rest until visibly calmed down again.

Note: In any shock situation you should have the Bach Flower Therapy Rescue Drops handy. Use two drops in 1 teaspoon of water, which you administer every 20 minutes into the side of the rabbit's mouth. Equally effective is the use of the homeopathic arnica C 30; use two drops in 1 teaspoon of water given once. Use a teaspoon or a syringe without a needle to administer these remedies into the side of the animal's mouth.

Indoor rabbits must be conditioned for outdoor living.

Warning Signs That Require Immediate Veterinary Care

Area of Observation	Symptom
Activity	• The animal is apathetic, retreats • Increased restlessness (with other symptoms)
Behavior	• Grinding teeth in pain • Stamping front paws • Circling and rolling • Abnormal posture • Trembling • Withdrawn in its cage, will not move
Eating Behavior	• Refuses foods • Eats well but loses weight
Breathing	• Quick, shallow breaths • Trembling • Shortness of breath • Coughing • Choking spasms
Head	• Held inclined • Animal shakes head
Ears	• Crusty deposits • Swollen, knotty bumps on skin
Eyes	• Loss of lively gleam • Appear dull and clouded
Nose	• Purulent discharge • The animal tries to rid itself of the discharge by snorting and pawing
Mouth	• Increased salivation
Abdomen	• The belly is tight and hard • The stomach is bloated, accompanied by severe pain when touched
Fur and Skin	• Hair loss, bald spots • Areas of inflammation, ulceration, swelling • Coat looks dull • Hair stands up
Digestive Tract	• Severe, watery, or blood-tinged diarrhea, sometimes very foul-smelling • Constipation that is not eased within two days (see page 56).

Coprophagy Reingestion

When you clean the cage you will notice—among the regular fecal pellets—some small, kidney-shaped, mucus-covered clusters of pellets. This is the nutrient-rich contents formed in the cecum of the rabbit's intestinal tract. Most rabbits ingest this nutritious fecal matter directly from the anal orifice. Only the excess is left in the bedding. Do not mistake this observation as a symptom of disease or abnormal behavior.

Greens and fresh foods are equally important as pellets for the daily meal plan.

Addresses and Literature

American Rabbit Breeders Association (ARBA)
P.O. Box 426
Bloomington, Illinois 61702
(309) 664-7500
Governs breed standards, registration, and
education.
Publishes: *Domestic Rabbits* magazine
On-line resources for guide books, pamphlets,
cage kits, and so on.
ARBAMAIL@aol.com

House Rabbit Society
1524 Benton Street
Alameda, California 94501
Publishes: *House Rabbit Journal*
All volunteer, nonprofit
www.rabbit.org

Countryside Publications, Ltd.
312 Portland Road
Highway 19 East
Waterloo, Wisconsin 53594
Publishes: *Rabbits* (a monthly magazine)

Books for Further Reading

Bennett, Bob, *Raising Rabbits the Modern Way,* Storey Communications, Pownal, VT, 1988.

Downing, Elisabeth, *Keeping Rabbits,* Pelham Books, London, 1979.

Harriman, M., *House Rabbit Handbook,* Drollery Press, Alameda, CA, 1991.

Hunter, Samantha, *Hop to It,* Barron's Educational Series, Inc., Hauppauge, NY, 1991.

National Research Council, *Nutrient Requirements of Rabbits,* 2nd edition, National Academy Press, Washington, DC, 1977.

Wegler, Monika, *Dwarf Rabbits,* Barron's Educational Series, Inc., Hauppauge, NY, 1998.

Wimmer, Paul, *A Beginner's Guide to Rabbits,* TFH Publications, Neptune City, NJ, 1986.

Author and Photographer

Monika Wegler has many years of experience with breeding and raising various rabbit breeds. She has authored and illustrated more than 30 pet books that are translated into many languages and for which she often created the photographs.

The Illustrator

György Jankovics studied graphic arts at the Art Conservatory in Budapest, Hungary, and in Hamburg, Germany. He has illustrated many books in this series and others, particularly on the subjects of animals and plants.

Photographs: Cover and Inside

Front cover: Dalmatian Rex doe (large photo); Dwarf, color (small photo).
Back cover: Rabbits love raised lookout locations, like this tree trunk.
Page 1: Rabbits look adorable when they wash their little faces.

Important Note

This book deals with the care and handling of rabbits. If injuries occur through scratches or bites, have your injuries medically treated. Chewing is a part of natural rabbit behavior. This makes supervision especially important when they run free in your home. These free runs are indispensable and should take place regularly. To avoid life-threatening accidents, be especially careful to see to it that your rabbits do not chew on electrical cords, thus suffering from electric shock.

Some people are allergic to rabbit hair. If you are not sure if you are, consult a physician.

Dwarf rabbits have very poor near vision, a problem that may find them frequently right under your feet. Be careful of rabbits continually running between your legs and accidentally tripping you because of their limited sight.

Pages 2–3: A rabbit and a puppy: An adult Dalmatian Rex and a Dalmatian puppy.
Pages 4–5: Friendship reaching across racial differences: On the left a Dwarf Lop, on the right a grown Deilenaar.
Pages 6–7: Two dwarf rabbits engaging in social grooming.
Page 64: My Abyssinian tom is close friends with our Deilenaar.

English translation © Copyright 1999 by Barron's Educational Series, Inc.
Original title of the book in German is *Kaninchen*
© Copyright 1998 by Gräfe und Unzer, Verlag GmbH, Munich

All inquiries should be addressed to:
Barron's Educational Series, Inc.
250 Wireless Boulevard
Hauppauge, NY 11788
http://www.barronseduc.com

Library of Congress Catalog Card No. 98-46003
International Standard Book No. 0-7641-0937-5

Library of Congress Cataloging-in-Publication Data
Wegler, Monika.
      [Kaninchen. English]
      Rabbits : everything about purchase, care, nutrition, grooming, behavior, and training / Monika Wegler ; photographs, Monika Wegler ; drawings, György Jankovics ; translated from the German by Helgard Niewisch.
         p. cm. — (A complete pet owner's manual)
      Includes bibliographical references and index.
      ISBN 0-7641-0937-5 (pbk.)
      1. Rabbits.   I. Title.   II. Series.
SF453.W4413   1999
636.932'2—dc21   98-46003
                                                            CIP

Printed in Hong Kong
9 8 7 6 5 4 3

1 Can I keep a large breed in the same way I would keep a small breed in my apartment?

Yes, the larger the rabbit, the larger the cage space and the more expenses you must anticipate.

2 Are there any particularly suitable breeds for outdoor living?

All breeds can adapt to year-round outdoor living as long as the housing is weatherproof and the animals are adapted beginning in the summer months.

3 I want to get another pet. What is the best companion pet for rabbits?

Most definitely, it is a guinea pig, which can be housed with the rabbit as long as the males are neutered. Guinea pigs and rabbits usually get along very well and live in harmony for years.

4 I have one rabbit and would like to get another. Will this work out?

Yes, but you need to be patient while getting them acquainted. Of course, there are exceptions to the rule.

5 At what age will my children be old enough for me to give them a rabbit?

By about the age of six a child can be taught to handle the rabbit properly.

An expert answers ten of the most commonly asked questions about keeping rabbits.